The Gift of Fire

Donated by

The Italian American Cultural Foundation

David Citino

The
Gift of
Fire

The University of Arkansas Press

Fayetteville 1986

Copyright © 1986 by David Citino
All rights reserved
Manufactured in the United States of America
Designer: Patricia Douglas Crowder
Typeface: Linotron 202 Trump
Typesetter: G & S Typesetters, Inc.
Printer: Thomson-Shore, Inc.
Binder: John H. Dekker & Sons, Inc.

Some of these poems first appeared in the following periodicals, often in slightly different form:

The Bennington Review	Modern Poetry Studies
The Centennial Review	Nimrod
The Greenfield Review	Ohio Journal
Hiram Poetry Review	The Ohio Review
The Hollins Critic	Poetry Northwest
Kansas Quarterly	Prairie Schooner
The Kenyon Review	South Dakota Review
The Literary Review	Southern Poetry Review
Michigan Quarterly Review	The Sun
Mid-American Review	Telescope
Mississippi Valley Review	Threepenny Review

I am grateful to The Ohio State University's Marion Campus, College of Humanities and Office of the Provost for awarding me a Special Research Assignment, during which some of the work that went into this book was done.

The paper used in this publication meets the minimum requirements of the American National Standard for Permanence of Paper for Printed Library Materials Z39.48—1984. ∞

LIBRARY OF CONGRESS CATALOGING-IN-PUBLICATION DATA

Citino, David, 1947–
  The gift of fire.
  I. Title.
PS3553.I86G5 1986   811'.54   85-16467
ISBN 0-938626-57-4
ISBN 0-938626-58-2 (pbk.)

*for Mary, Nathan, Dominic, Maria
and all my other teachers*

Contents

I. *The Gift of Fire*
    Dust, Ash, Pine, and Dust Again   3
    How to Wonder, How to Love   4
    The Gift of Fire   6
    The Dead Forever Dead   7
    He Shows the People What to Do with the Dead   8
    Letter from the Shaman: The Tribe with No Myth   9
    Cleveland, Angels, Ogres, Trolls   11
    Volare   12
    Sitting in the Sixth Grade at Ascension of Our Lord School in Cleveland, Ohio, Reading a Pamphlet Entitled *Possession in Iowa*   14
    The Date   15
    Guadalcanal, Feldspar, Sleeping with My Wife   17
    The Funeral   18
    My Son's Violin   19
    Learning to Fly   20
    The Signature   21
    Flying into Billings to Read My Poetry   23
    On the Photograph in *Paris Match* of Anna and Maria, Siamese Twins   24
    China Opens to the Western World   25
    Nightly News and Summer Drive   26
    Changing the World   28

II. *Lives of the Saints*
    Christina the Astonishing, Virgin   31
    Besarian   32
    The Last Words of Juan de la Cruz   33
    Francis Meets a Leper   34
    Robert Falcon Scott Writes to His Wife from Antarctica, March 29, 1912   35
    Father Coughlin   36
    A Letter from Delmore   37
    The Pastor's Creed   39

        The Pastor Praises the Creator   40
        The Pastor on Comparative Religions   41
        Man Offers to Take Messages to Dead   42

III. *Einstein, Placenta, the Caves of Lascaux*
        Principles of Scarcity, Doctrines of Growth   45
        The Observer Alters the Observed by the Act of
            Observation   46
        Lecture to the Bioscience Class: Pine and Lightning,
            Cataclysm and Stone   47
        The Sea of Kansas, Ohio Tundra, Time Still
            Running Out   48
        The History of Wood   49
        On the Nature of the Beast   50
        Einstein, Placenta, the Caves of Lascaux   51
        The Bird Graveyard   52

The Gift of Fire

I.

The Gift of Fire

Dust, Ash, Pine, and Dust Again

The first woman, the first man
were made of dust. They'd not
the resolve to stand firm together
through tantrums of the seasons,
weren't flexible enough to take shade
when God hung his blazing sun too near.
They came apart in the first drizzle,
merest winds scattering them forever.

The next woman, the next man
were made of ash and pine. They were
too stiff to reach out for one another.
Growing too hot, cold, they warped.
Striving too close, they withered, paled.
They were too kind. Birds, ants
took advantage. Dogs. The first storm
drove them crazy, blasted them to stumps.

God was lessoned by these mistakes.
The next woman, the next man were made
of bones lashed artfully with sinew,
covered with hair and skin tough enough
to endure three score years and ten
of weather. And to honor their parents
when they cease to be, they're buried
in wood and made to come to dust again.

How to Wonder, How to Love

In the beginning God made us from what
He found strewn around, gnarl and knot
of root, bark, trunk, ocean's wrack and pearl,
spittle and froth, coolness of stone,
heat of ooze beneath forest's mold and spore,
shards of hoarfrost spangling each field.

He gave us the gift of five senses,
and to keep us wishing every day for night
and night for day, a sixth, the ache to know
Him, want to hear and scent, savor and feel,
look Him in the eye, this gift our art.
Then He went and hid, and with our hands

we set about carving an altar from each stone,
hewing cathedrals from the trees, painting
the world with the shade of our own blood,
ash and soot of every kind of wood, fire
of sacrifice, flower, grain and fruit.
We filled the world with figures of God

fashioned from what we found strewn around:
God of mountain thunder, flood and wind,
God of blood, ewe and ram, dung and jewel,
climb and fall, vine and terebinth, God
of slither, hop and leap, of soar, God
hacked to pieces, hunks of crimson meat,

God reassembled, circle made of arcs, of wholes,
new as spark, ash-old, quick as lust, hate,
of quiver and shaft, spear and prey, pine
and sky, God of penis and volcano, vagina
and fountainhead, lemur God, scarab God, crow
and crocodile, plow and furrow, seed and bee,

of stamen and pistil, estrus and silky seed,
God who eats the light of every day and spits
it out again, God the gesture and sign,
steps to every dance, wind of all right words,
right of rites, God of bright myths hung
in night skies, God the darkness that defines

each light, as many Gods as stars, sounds,
sights, textures, tastes, scents and hues,
as many as fingerprints, shapes of snowflakes.
The art and soul He gave us when He made us
make and break Him over and over until we learn
in time to dream and wonder, how to love.

The Gift of Fire

When Trickster saw that God
fashioned the first woman and man
from clay with great care,
pain of cramped fingers,
light of squinting eyes,
and that he painted their faces
in his own image
and baked them in his kiln
until they were done,
breathing hot life between their lips,

and when Trickster saw that God
placed them on the teeming earth unclothed
and sent reckless, variable winds
to snap their limbs
and floods to bloat their bellies
with pestilence, fire to burn away
the inside of bone, breast, lung
and strip them of their perfect flesh
he made a plan,
and held his belly and laughed,

and the laughter became
a tree that came apart in time
to nourish a grove
that came apart in time
to foster a great forest
that grew to cover all the land.
And walking there woman and man
found shelter from all four winds,
timber to fashion home, weather floods,
and, blossoming from holy wood,

the gift of fire.

The Dead Forever Dead

Trickster, so life always will mean
and there will be sufficiency,
hellgrammite and trout, ponies and fields,
makes himself an invisible fire
and visits the tent of one who's
just fallen, slowly burns away
flesh from muscle, sinew from bone,
the very marrow boiling away
so that, while most children
are permitted to become old,
and most of the sick to grow whole again,
no matter how many tears fall
from eyes of mothers, lovers,
daughters and sons, no matter
how deeply the still one's kin
gash their faces, how many lips
are parted by curses and prayers
all the dead must stay forever dead.

He Shows the People What to Do with the Dead

Almost from the beginning they got
in the way, lying in crowded tents
staring at young ones and old, cold
as wind over a broken tooth, littering
battlefields until the warriors couldn't step,
sitting up against lodgepoles in the councils
with nothing to say. So the people
stuck them in shallow holes, no more
than corn-deep, but at the next harvest
they came back. No one, not even their mothers,
wanted them, because the people who lived
couldn't live staring death in the face.
Because the dead forgot even how to take
a joke. Because of flies. Trickster
had a plan. He taught the tribe to plant
the dead at least a man's height
beneath the ground, too deep to spring back,
gave them mourning songs and tales
to ease the wait for grass to grow back
over the mounds, taught them the art
of tears to nourish fields and seas,
grew them flowers and trees to sweeten
the air above every city of the dead
and created hummingbirds and bees to preserve
the sweetness of night forever. He put
the dead out of sight at the edge of the mind
so that even after numberless grandparents,
bark and wail of seasons being slaughtered,
death still comes as the great surprise.

Letter from the Shaman: The Tribe with No Myth

In their territory there lived
no gods or consorts, seraphim or trolls,
no sky-father or earth-mother.
Snakes were snakes, women women
and men no more or less.
Rivers, tors and groves were mere features
of topography. Those few who cared
to gaze into the sky at night
would do so, no questions asked.
They understood that the moon
waxed and waned for no apparent reason
but science, and the stars
spinning at random formed
quite by accident what other tribes
in their frenzied stupors
swore were signs, prey and hunter,
lovers, haters, daughters and sons.
The earth perhaps was flat,
perhaps not. What did it matter
in the end? Folk without lore,
no one could remember. They recognized
no grandparents among the beasts and birds:
some were good to eat; some not;
while others were to be feared
purely for practical reasons,
poison, talon, crush and fang.
They made no distinction between raw, cooked.
Time didn't count. Dreams never meant.
Coming of age was precisely when
the night before the hairless young
couldn't bleed or grow erect as spears,
couldn't conceive, while the day after
they could. Their fires burned slowly,
with no stories to feed the flames.
When it came time for them to go

there was no talk of planting,
no songs of fear or yearning
they would rise to walk again
among the living. Their dead were dead.
In this land lovers loved
because it seemed a good idea,
all things being equal.
Patternless, drifting from one fire
to the next, one coupling,
the tribe came apart, each woman and man
rational as hell, creatures
of wandering. And their children
wander among us still today,
drifting, missing but not quite lost.

Cleveland, Angels, Ogres, Trolls

> *Drumcliff and Rosses and choke-full of ghosts. By bog, road, rath, hillside, sea border, they gather in all shapes: headless women, men in armor, shadow hares, fire-tongued hounds, whistling seals and others. A whistling seal sank a ship the other day.*—Yeats, The Celtic Twilight

Still today, sober and tenured as I can be,
I go back. When I close my eyes it's Cleveland,
I've fallen out of puberty, lost the beast's
rough hair and heavy hurt. Angels go with me.
To be means giving credence without question.
The mirror's a miracle even before I take off
my clothes. Aunts work wonders
with their crazy praying. Novenas shatter glasses
poised in palsied hands of drunks, the lame
leap and whirl like windy leaves. Kennedy
comes back, Jackie at his side unbloodied,
his skull smooth and whole as the schoolroom globe.
Old men stop by to sharpen scissors or haggle
for the family's rags, their carts powered by song.
We pray for the conversion of Russia.
The whole world's Catholic, it rains new babies
every night, nothing in the world's to be
discounted and hordes of children meet each day
to learn to do and say, eyes glowing streetlamp bright
with currents of perfect fear, all joy.
Nothing tastes the same. Ogres and trolls
patrol the dark beneath each bed. Where I step
glaciers have been and may come again.
Tomorrow the sun will rise forever.

Volare

Just as lights inside our living room
and steam from water boiling on the stove
erase Cleveland from the picture window,
father comes in,
stands in the kitchen, one shoulder thrust forward,
feet apart the way he's seen Lanza stand,
eyelids drooping like Dean Martin's or Como's,
Lucky Strike stuck to lower lip.
*We can leave the confusion
and all disillusion behind.*
And we know he got the raise,
his laborer's share of chemical company profits
from the Manhattan Project
and the revolution in plastics.
Four hundred a year. And that's not hay.
He grabs my mother
and spins with her before the stove,
wooden spoon brandished like the fine lady's fan
she saw that day in pages of *Life*.
*Just like birds of a feather
a rainbow together we'll find.*
Then he comes for me,
and I'm soaring above cauldrons
of rigatoni and sauce bubbling bright
as the scarlet cassocks altar boys wear
at Christmas and Easter.
He brings me back to earth
and twirls away to phone his mother.
That night when he comes home from moonlighting
in the credit department at Sears,
feet heavy as bricks,
he'll come to my bedroom and tell me again
how there'll be no promotion for him
because he couldn't go to college
but still he's risen higher than his father

who put in fifty years with the B & O.
He'll step out the door
and for a moment his head will be caught in light
like some raptured hoary saint drunk on love
in the window of Ascension of Our Lord
and the last thing I'll hear
will be his lovely forlorn baritone
fading, falling into stillness.
Volare. Wo-wo. Cantare. Wo-o-o-o.

Sitting in the Sixth Grade at Ascension of Our Lord School in Cleveland, Ohio, Reading a Pamphlet Entitled *Possession in Iowa*

This was a new catechism, a new testament.
I looked at the page and saw the farm girl soar
above the disordered brass bed, agile as a fly,
cling naked to the ceiling while in the doorway
her mother, shapeless as bread dough in a sad print dress,
sobbed noiselessly into a ruffled apron, father
having long before fled to the barn to hammer something
heavy and loud. Where did the girl learn
the good church Latin she used to curse
the pudgy German pastor come to purge her?
Who taught her to revile his shiny pants and black shoes
in a sow's squeal that raised the hackles
under the soiled collar, taught her the very thing
to say about his mother and a host of beasts,
to stare at a point below his belt and wet her lips
until he squirmed, and ran to call the Jesuits?
I read on, the rows of bean and corn
filling with weeds on all four horizons beyond
the weathered wooden house, the windmill gone mad,
neighbors clustered in the yard among clucking hens,
praying softly to hear every word, crows
chuckling above. Who made this? Why? And the girl,
when it was over was she another Dorothy back
in Kansas, bored with tiresome farmhands
and going nowhere? And at forty, harsh blond hair
beehived on her head, breasts supported by wires,
wearing clothes too girlish, running to fat and prone
to cry for no reason? I wondered about her,
and all the things that might be without being seen.

The Date

That night, blue and gold in my Ignatius H.S. jacket,
varsity *I* blocked on my breast, I said goodbye
to Mother and Father, stepping between them
and the handsome, concerned anchorman, and left rattling

in the green Ford wagon, the Savior fastened to the dash
with a magnet, Harshaw Chemical Co. sticker glowing
on the windshield, streets of Cleveland leading me,
potholed like the moon, urgent voices loud all around:

Just because you've become a young man, now,
There's still some things that you don't understand
now. . . . Keep your freedom for as long as you can now.
Miracles. By degrees the neat West Side lawns sloped

toward the writhing Cuyahoga, rank and viscous
in its dark bed, its load of sin moving slowly
into Erie past ore boats and mills, pillars of salt
and taconite high enough to hide heaven, sand dunes.

Scents of sulfur, dead crappie, sheepshead, winds of forges
driving me toward the Heights. I followed the lake
chased by herring gulls heavy from the dump, on the
    windshield
fragile Canadian soldiers exhausted from their love,

legs jigging in wind, *danse macabre.* Too soon I was there.
The instant before she opened the door I saw reflected
in the pane a face old as hell, wrinkled and worn
like a downtown wino's suit, my glasses thick

as February ice smoothing over Erie's Ice Age scar,
hair white as the breath of a child running home in fear
through vacant lots. Then she was there, seventy-five
if she was a day, pleated skirt, knee socks, saddle shoes,

neat white nuns' school blouse bunched at the tiny waist,
ponytail smooth and gray as ancient sidewalk slate,
fingers gnarled, both of us holding our faces
and screaming at the one great horror, just our age.

Guadalcanal, Feldspar, Sleeping with My Wife

I'm surprised to learn my bed's grown
no larger. Father tells me again
how on Guadalcanal when the Japanese would scream
from the trees "To hell with Roosevelt,"
he'd bellow back at the jungle night
"Hirohito's diddling your mothers."
Mother shows me my model planes,
Zero, Stuka, B-26, still held together
with drops of glue pale as semen.
She shows me my comics of the Korean Conflict:
Die, Imperialist Warmonger! Eat lead, Gook!
I learn from him that Gulf Oil's taking over
the chemical industry, the company
he's worked for thirty years.
He quotes me the price of a thousand wood pallets,
a boxcar of feldspar, a shipload
of South African chrome. He says over and over
the world's come apart since V–J Day,
and Truman should've let MacArthur cross over
into China. She shows me "in case anything
should happen" where she's hidden the strongbox,
envelopes stuffed with savings bonds, one
for every payday, curls from my first haircut
still soft as pages of my St. Joseph Daily Missal.
Silently, they accuse me of making them old,
forgetting everything important,
sleeping with my wife.

The Funeral

When you need them most, to ask
where to go from here, your hair
growing sparse as February grass,
they've gone, singly or united
under stone in the safest place
where the stranger who cares for them,
pulling a mower behind his International Harvester
to trim the grass they vivify,
setting poison out for mice and squirrels
that mate nearby, for weeds,
knows them better than you, seasons
laboring by like old city buses against the wind
but too far away to disturb
a parent's rest, their reward for teaching you
that being their child's the same
as being no one else, that mourning them's
the final thing you have to learn.

My Son's Violin

Hard as he tries, he can't get it right.
The house writhes; Bach lurches
through the rooms like a drunk.
My son carries the instrument delicately,
as if it were something holy, older
than he can imagine. He winces
as I clasp it, roughly pluck and hear,
twist and twist again until my hands
have fashioned the order my father
made for me: E A D G. Everything's
right again, he tells me with his eyes.
He thanks me and goes out, footsteps
growing dim as he mounts the stairs.
All at once the house lifts and spins
with music. If it were given to me
to choose, this would be the moment
of my death.

Learning to Fly

I step into dawn's song, each tree a ladder
to heaven, Ohio the loveliest noise. I move
through the parking lot of Harding High
just as light ignites shattered bottles
of Stroh's and Little Kings Ale, treasures
unearthed from the fossil record of night.
Sun rainbows oil slicks from 200 near-wrecks
that again today will bear to school burdens
of youth, lovers paired in front seat and back
moving above the earth to passionate static,
symphony of generation, hearts in flight.

The birds trill their names into the chill
of March, each living thing crying out
for love. Thrush and song sparrow run
their scales, robin and redbird chanting matins,
dove's hoot, whistle and moan, every one
aching to be made two, two, two. I'm amazed
at such eloquence. How could I forget
in just one winter such bold notes? Here
are angels of bone and flesh beating hearts
against frigid dawn, creatures of light
who through their yearning learn to fly.

The Signature

> *A man's writing seems to be a part of his very flesh and bones; he cannot discard it at will.*—A. S. Osborn, Questioned Documents

It's the many ways this name's been made
concerns me now. Grandfather's *Michele*
remade as Cleveland's *Mike*. Father's *Giovanni*
rewritten as World War Two *Johnny*. Map
of the way from them, then to here and now.
Infant I's left hand index finger stirring wind,
pebbles and sand, bright wood blocks.
Laddie pencil's grievous weight bearing down hard
on gray wide-lined paper, circumference
gripped in a miniscule fist feeling big
as the handle of the Louisville Slugger
signed *Larry Doby*. The scowling nun
hiding under some holy alias making my name
on the board under the heading *Misbehavers*.
My mother calling from unlettered chaos,
David, David. Chalk on sidewalk, brick.
Broken heart, my initials and another's,
blood-drops oozing from the wound
of Cupid's arrow thrusting through.
Crayola points that endured just one printing,
then were struck dumb. *Color inside
the lines*, my teachers insisted.
Impossible, the lines fine as webs strung
between June's dawn trees, my eyes still
without the lenses that would tutor them
in intricacies of earth, windy forsythia,
unprinted snow, rippled glint of lake face,
every distant address. Chalk-holders,
forging lines of penmanship and song.
*O my name is MacNamara I'm the leader
of the band*. Fountain pens, blue stain
spreading in pockets of blouses and shirts

above every eighth-grade heart. Bulbs and levers
to replenish fluid indelible as blood.
Eradicator's bleachy stench, my left hand
smearing letters of the name the priests
promised would be written forever.
Back of the sandlot uniform, just above
my name and number, *Corrigan's Funeral Home.*
It's the name concerns me now, praenomen
and cognomen, as just beyond the stenciled door,
Lawyers Title Inc., across from the smiling woman
who's handed me the ballpoint
saying *Sign please where I've put the X,*
at the signing for our first house,
massive basswood's heart-shaped leaves
and papery winged fruit whispering its own name
to wind, half-acre of Ohio we'll lie
and say we own, a thirty-year debt,
with careful hand I fashion again
the letters of my name.

Flying into Billings to Read My Poetry

I've been lifted out of my life,
earth spinning beneath, to be
set down to sing in another place
both two hours earlier and later,
Rocky Mountain Time, than this time
in Ohio. Everyone I know's become

an old hit tune, those I love
a stirring around the heart,
below the belt. This cold and high
even Chicago seems like a good idea.
Those going with me, dressed for cattle,
geology or skiing, know exactly

what time it is, every other wrist
ticking the mountains away, moments
of one hundred and twelve lives.
If they knew that in my suitcase
in the belly of this beast I'd stashed
one hundred poems, which of them

would jump me from behind, hold me
until all of us were safe on earth?
One disaster away from everything
I've planned, the Northwest Orient jet
circles Billings for the approach,
its shadow, the priceless portrait

of the priceless space we make in air,
racing Montana's lunar terrain
for the runway. I pray for a world
where we all get our money's worth.
What was it made me dream I could fly?
Foolish enough to want to sing to strangers?

On the Photograph in *Paris Match* of Anna and Maria, Siamese Twins
Deux têtes mais un seul coeur.

In the same issue as the Pope's
nodding, mitred progress through Asia,
President Marcos' head bowed under the weight
of corruption like a pious beggar's,
his bride's glittering just behind his,
heavy with rouge, hair spray, pearls,

the same issue where a colonel,
fascist, mustached in a comic-opera hat,
waves his pistol in the Spanish Assembly,
bald heads of legislators rising
from behind their desks like moons
from evening mountains, you lie.

Face to face in the incubator,
two perfect heads where our eyes tell us
only one can be, nature's gross miscalculation,
No grafted to *Yes.* One spinal column,
set of legs, arms, one heart and sex
but forever of two minds. Closer

than lovers but never enough. Given
the gravity of this world, demands made
on one small heart, the prognosis isn't good.
One face, serene, dreams; the other
contorts with fiercest weeping. You mean
all things precious to us, little ones,

pretty monster of love.

China Opens to the Western World

I want to meet the Chinese, to learn
what they feel walking through garden mists
at the instant of sunrise, say to one another
in tea shops, in the fields, how their rooms smell
as they prepare supper, how children there
speak of parents when they're alone with friends.
But Richard Nixon goes instead.
Julie and David Eisenhower. Susan Anton.
The presidents of the Big Ten universities.
Sales reps for Coke and Mountain Dew.
The entire cast of *The Love Boat.*
The Chinese people are offended to see
great legs, great breasts uncovered,
television actors and actresses embracing,
kissing with open mouths before the cameras.
I want them to see instead the utter loveliness
of my grandmother as she'd bend over
the kitchen sink and hold each dish close
as she could to the eyes in which glaucoma
slowly was putting out the light, explain
to them how one-third of a century after my birth
into post-war days of demon and angel
I'm still learning to trust the dark,
how I've never known real hunger,
never held a weapon in anger, tell them
that my wife and I've planted our garden,
a plot just long and broad enough
to contain us while our children blossom,
glistening with their own dawn. "It certainly *is*
a great wall," Mr. Nixon states.
His words make history.

Nightly News and Summer Drive

The window glows with a world
where every man's a uniform or shroud,
every child weeps, no planes
touch ground safely, no storefront
stands uncharred. And then the bodies
bloated like parade balloons, haloed
with flies. The P.L.O. claims
"indiscriminate attacks on civilians
by U.S.-made Israeli rockets and jets."
The Israelis blame "atrocities
by Palestinian terrorists
against women and children."
Lebanese mothers wail like sirens,
lift hands to the cameraman, pray
to the U.N. A spokesman
for the President of the United States
says that today's sudden turn of events,
"while not unexpected given
the Soviet Union's unceasing efforts
to exploit a volatile situation
is nevertheless to be deplored
by peace-loving peoples everywhere."
I press the button that brings back darkness,
gather my sons for a drive into Ohio's
countryside, earth furrowed boundlessly
in moral maize and green, air we can breathe.
We pass Harding's home, where a world
once met to pray for *normalcy,* and farther
his tomb, stark as Stonehenge, erected
by the nation's schoolchildren, tarnished Doughboy
leaning toward the new stone map of Vietnam
paid for by the Disabled American Veterans,
Firebase Marion. My sons, seated
behind me in the car, stare placidly
out the window,

trusting me as they'll trust no other.
I must get them out of town,
and they're certain I know the way,
but all roads seem suddenly strange
and far as I can see
through every intersection ahead
light after light
burns red.

Changing the World
for Marguerite Guzman Bouvard

Ohio stiffens slowly in its Christmas rigor,
dies on our lips like a bad idea, its foundries
many degrees too cold, grain bins many bushels
too full. *16% Unemployment in Cuyahoga County,*
the *Plain Dealer* screams silently. *19% in Marion,*
Harding's *Star* replies. Security guards
check locks and chains keeping a million workers
from their tools. Mines and assembly lines
lie unoccupied, forklifts undriven. Big rigs.
Cleveland stevedores swing cranes over freighters
registered to Liberia, unload Japanese steel
while fifty ore boats ride high at river moorings.

Russian Backfire bombers buzz U.S. carriers
off Alaska's fragile shore. Hundreds, thousands
of Soviet and Afghan troops are buried forever
under crumbling mountains. Basques and Bulgarians
plot to incinerate the Pope. Belfast. Beirut.
All over the country power plants with faulty welds
tick, glow. Parents, our own, grow too small
for us to find them, forget our names, prepare
for a long journey. Our daughters and sons
sit at night in automobiles with steamed windows
plotting their future, believing dark's a friend,
studying the love they think can change the world.

II.

Lives of the Saints

Christina the Astonishing, Virgin

Death's stone rolled away from mouth and eyes,
she jerked upright in the open coffin
during Requiem, dressed in clothes
she was to wear to heaven. The place emptied
in seconds, mourners thundering down aisles
pursued by the one fate worse than death,
the priest gulping bread and wine
as he stumbled out the door. Their fear,
at once foreign and familiar, lingered,
a pall, a scream inside her head.
She was the sorriest thing on earth.
"I've been to paradise, lain with angels," she swore.
"Why've I been brought back? What time
is it? What's that awful smell?"
She sought apart—in belfry and burrow,
currents far enough from shore for her
to be able to dream of no one else,
mountain crags softened by wildflower, pine,
ovens warm with loaves that rose like miracles—
a parole from earth's bony penitentiary.
Naked in the baptismal font, scrubbing flesh
until it bled, she ached for a world
cleansed by forty days of rain, plagues
of locust, brimstone. It seemed
she was always downwind of somebody,
and when there was no wind the odor was there
stronger than ever, bodies living
as they died, cloying essence of the begotten,
urgent perfume of decay.

Besarian

> *Fearing a nocturnal emission, the monk Besarian didn't lie down for forty years.*

Brother, you saw all around
women and men beaten down to darkness
again and again before their time
by gravity's cruel, senseless rain,
a world inclined to love, at rest
from weight of a long day's shifting light,
the attraction of spinning bodies.

It wasn't for you to cut off
in one stroke the foaming beast,
as Origen did, and bury it
while spirit slumbered, endured, numb.
That would be too easy, an act of will
alone, one irrevocable thrust. Sleepless,
you stood more hurt, chronic ache

of splintered shin, broken arch,
throbbing knots of calf, back, thigh.
Upright, you could stand for experience,
night's bracing beauty, knowing
the reward awaiting you at the end:
rest after a long day's vigilance,
earth above and beneath you like a lover.

The Last Words of Juan de la Cruz

Those broken moaning things—bandaged
to hide their sex and other wounds—
in the Hospital of the Tumors in Medina,
dying because it's easy to love too well,
taught me the sadness, bitter as vinegar,
a long life ferments in the cask of the soul.
To be anything over-long means to know
the stench and mortal pain of everything human.
To love too much means to end up hating,
disappointed as an old fire, territory
of its lost wealth marked darkly all around.
When Simon of Kent, my Carmelite father,
learned this he shut himself in a hollow oak
for twenty years. Berthold, crusader
of Calabria, tried to make his way to heaven
by climbing Mount Carmel. I ask my brothers
to beat me, to make it easier to refuse
their love. I wear chains beneath my robe
to show the hold of earth's gravity on those
who live just for the light. Already flesh grows
over iron. Soon enough I'll be free. Lonely
in any tongue means holy. When everybody sings
it's too hard to understand the words.

Francis Meets a Leper

He heard the bell toll, erratic
in a palsied hand, and smelled
the goatish scent before he saw
the figure moving in mist on the road
to Assisi, a traveler gloved and shod,
as was the law, to hide the sores,
a man's inhumanity, missing fingers
and toes, and tried to unmask the face,
slack muscles showing nothing
but astonishment, lower lids keeping
eyes open always to our providential decay,
flesh soft and thick as rotten wood.
Francis saw in bleary eyes, near to him
as his mother's as she loved him,
a brother, then someone dearer, wrapped
as he'd seen others in his father's cloth
that first had profited English shepherds
and the weavers of Ghent, a skin
bleached white as bone, a flower blazing
in snow, so close to perfection it could
only decay. Francis did the only thing
he could, sun rising high enough now
to burn away the mist. He unwrapped
the face, studying lineaments fashioned
by a master's hand, image and likeness
of the death that beautifies all living.
He closed his eyes and kissed.

Robert Falcon Scott Writes to His Wife from Antarctica, March 29, 1912

Promise me you'll see to it our son's more strenuous.

At the end of this world we've nearly traveled
only cold's for certain, the heart at its destination
surging, then slowing in weariness, blood spun
in wind's centrifuge, latticed with crystal.
In time our surfaces become sculpture, holding
the last gesture, undecayable by law, my widow.

My two companions arrived first, now lie together
in this stiffened tent on the Great Ice Barrier
eleven miles from one ton of pemmican and oil,
like lovers whose passions were so perfectly conducted
they became an art, limbs open for all time,
lips blue and parted, flesh turgid, tongues.

I write to signify miscalculations, accomplishments—
stopping in force-five gales to warm with black fingers
the dying dogs, ponies and men, and trying
to reckon under clouds that seemed unfathomable,
dragging along fossil rocks even as we dried
to fossil rock in wintering airs, the awesome glare.

In these horizonless vistas beauty drove us blind.
I write because all of us are faced with the prospect
of letters unformed, meanings unsigned, erasures,
and in this ice country we've failed into every line
holds its shape, every sound its timbre and pitch.
I write because it's cold, love, the only reason after all.

Father Coughlin

While the Great Hunger gusts across dust-rich fields
and depressed city streets strewn with handbills,
crumpled manifestoes, forty million believers
sit in living rooms on meatless Sunday afternoons
imagining his eyes glowing red as radio tubes.

*A revolution in this country by 1933 unless
we wake up. Bolshevik councils in the Ford plants.*

Practicing in the mirror to perfect each gesture
and arched brow, he screams at himself, names
names, bankers and lawyers who rule world and word
with the help of Franklin Delano Rosenfeld.
He packs a pearl-handled Smith & Wesson
to protect himself from plutocrats who eat the poor.

*Modern banking's the big crap shoot. Roosevelt's
a Kerensky, dupe, Judas, liar: the Great Scab.*

He brings Babe Ruth to church to increase attendance,
praises the Führer because he makes the Germans
forget about sex, accuses godless Stalin
of bankrolling the pornography Catholic boys
lock themselves in the bathroom with. Even the Pope
fears the metallic hysteria crackling through the air.

*Britain martyred ten million sons of Erin, now
drops bombs on eighty-eight million German Christians.*

One hundred clerks open his mail. Politicians beg
to be pictured at his side. As pitiless winds
whistle through cracks in old brick, the poor
hear the disembodied voice shrill as sirens urging them
to take back the streets, blame someone for their pain.

A Letter from Delmore
A page a day! no day without a page!
So must I pay attention to myself.

The other day in the stinking bar dark
as Plato's cave you didn't know me right away?
The shape of my head's been changed drastically.

You don't know what it's like to fear
that if clatter of mind and soul gets louder
you'll shatter, leaving only shards of promise.

I spent my first marriage at the movies.
For my wife the sex act was only an act, and I'd
always rather type, or dream the real thing.

"Fuck the Jews," a Harvard boy told me one day
after class because I rejected his themes. To be
artist and Jew, to correspond with Eliot and Pound

and watch them falter, coming apart in time, means
summoning up ghosts real as wreaths poets make
of their apartness, every damned birthday.

Each night, unconscious in bed, the body grows,
the nails, hair sprouting about the face and sex,
dinner miracled to blood. So much transpires

I simply can't conduct. Why don't I feel as much
for poetry as I do for the Giants? Nubile girls
who follow me home from class, short of breath

for my great lies? I spend my days writing letters
to Socrates and Adlai, Milton and Rimbaud,
chewing Dexedrine like peanuts, jam jar of gin

my chalice. I should be making plans to get up
every dawn, see the light, take vitamins, smoke
only pipes, get to the gym, beg forgiveness

of those whose lives I've misspoken. But it's
a free country. Who says everyone must be happy?
Face it. Even paranoids have real enemies.

JFK, Rockefeller and the Pope, I know, are seeing
my wife, meeting her at the Polo Grounds
to conspire against me, all of them in dark glasses,

plotting to decipher me while all that's good in life
unfolds on the green and brown field. My analyst
says I've fallen for myself. Too hard. Who knows?

The mirror exceeds my eloquence with its own.
Each day's a novel no one can read. Please write
to assure me you've understood every word.

The Pastor's Creed

Michelangelo's dead wrong. Adam had no navel.
He was born unattached.

Frogs come spontaneously from Nile mud. A woman and man
can burst into flame for no reason at all.

Swans, silent all their lives, sing like the devil
when Death splashes toward them. So should we.

Lemmings are the wisest of creatures, most realistic.
Bees die of sorrow to learn they've caused hurt.
Wolves lust after the flesh of young brides.

Teeth, nails and hair ignore the reaper, grow
till Judgment Day. Quicklime in time
returns all beauty to dust. A body falling
from a many storied height's dead before it touches earth.

Because they're gotten with a greater enthusiasm,
bastards make better artists, lovers, priests, saviors.

God striped the melon to make it easier for father
to cut it into equal slices.

Unwary women can get into trouble in bath water,
during dreams, in the stable, before any mirror.

Drinking from a garden hose fills the belly
with snakes. Birth hurts. Love. Death. God made
Eve's pelvis narrow enough to squeeze her children's heads,
to teach them life's a series of constraints;
narrow enough to pleasure Adam in the night, to give him
a preview of paradise. When an old woman falls
her pelvis shatters, to illustrate the gravity of age.

Wars are good for religion, religion for wars.

This life of desperation soon must end. Thus we must learn
to rejoice, to mourn.

There are more extinct than living species.
More corpses than lovers.

The Pastor Praises the Creator

Dearly beloved, I mean today
to praise the God who gave the tribes
wine, the crisp flesh of suckling pig,
then told them "Thou must not."

Who gave them swords and ploughshares,
lambs and lions, demons and redeemers.
Who made half of them like pestles,
half like mortars, then told them

in themselves they were complete.
Cool soothing fingers and fevers
between the legs. Reason and gooseflesh,
curtains and candles, lightning and oak,

seven days to live and as many sins,
lungs and mold, books and blind men, veins
and age. Who fashioned them a harvest home,
then created wanderlust and roads.

The Pastor on Comparative Religions

When Druids took the names of trees and stones
and hidden parts of the body and made them
letters of their alphabet, carpenters and masons
became poets, and lovers learned all songs by heart.

Wenceslas the Emperor roasted a cook who made him meat
too well done, pissed in the baptismal font
because he knew his water was holier. At fourteen
every peasant girl in his kingdom became a woman
in his rite of pain, and tears became blood by law.

Urban VIII poisoned all the birds in Rome
because the music of their flight and fright kept him
from prayer and soothing music of the spheres.
He arrested Galileo for the same reason.

Like bread dough, the dead will rise if you flail them,
pierce them with the sign of the cross, knead them
just long enough, place them in the dark behind stone.

Cotton Mather found a witch anywhere there was
no fire. Mother Ann Lee discovered a serpent
in her husband's nightclothes. To Joseph Smith
perdition was the state of Missouri.
To Adam, Abraham and Moses, God the Father and Son,
Mohammed and the Buddha, to be alone was hell.
To Houdini, it was every place still and dark enough
for him to hear his mother calling.

Man Offers to Take Messages to Dead

A man with an incurable brain tumor promises to deliver messages to the dead at $20 a missive.—Associated Press

By now, how many must there be?
Since Abel went down
in his mad brother's field—
hundreds of googols of them?
A googolplex or more, given
all the messiahs, captains and kings,
the minor functionaries
who couldn't refuse an order?
They must come in minute by minute
from everywhere, especially
the Middle East, sub-Sahara,
Friday night Cleveland and Detroit,
earthquake, plane crash,
that stretch of Ohio 423.
However many, however long
it takes, tell them all,
rabble to bluebloods,
every daughter and son
that I'm beginning to recognize
how the sum of their names
is a music
something like love.

III.

Einstein, Placenta, the Caves of Lascaux

Principles of Scarcity, Doctrines of Growth

Research shows that for each discovery
of alternative sources of energy, every breakthrough
in the necessary technology,
countless mechanical things go haywire or quit,
valves and gears rusting open or shut
like mouths of palsied old men
wetting their trousers on benches in a city park,
needles of meters dancing like charismatics,
ticking into danger zones, silicon chips struck
senseless, forgetting their binary creed,
not knowing bit from byte, tapes erased,
screens dark. It's estimated by official sources
high in the Secretariat of the U.N. that rates
of global cruelty and rage continue
to grow geometrically while understanding
plods along in the achingly slow human way,
one plus one means two.
We've got incontrovertible proof
that for every candle matched to stay
night's Ice Age a power grid goes down
along some seaboard, the albino squirrel
it took all time to make
blasted to ash in the great transformer,
a galaxy trembling like a gypsy moth in hail
that speaks one last time its perfect colors
then falls, every dawn the awful fatal wound.

The Observer Alters the Observed by the Act of Observation
—*Heisenberg's Uncertainty Principle*

This road finds its way to dawn,
river of particles, current of waves,
take your pick. Nebulous and concrete
as my own death. Ohio 315 mimics the writhe
of the Olentangy, water shimmering pavement
always just ahead, tires dry as bleached bone.
In such August madness, nothing's what
it means. Even fields are ephemera, soil
a few months ago, now flourishing bean
stubbled with pigweed, cornstalks rising
to volunteer, in the next field cornrows
high enough to lift all four horizons
behind roadside chicory stuttering its blue,
palsied in wakes of velocity and mass.
I remember the times I've wakened a lover
perfect in still beauty. What we touch or taste
we alter. Thoreau wearing a path from cabin
to pond's edge. *What's missing from this picture?*
we were asked as children. *He, she, it. I am.
Act as if I were looking over your shoulder,*
my mother would say as I left in the family car
to perform experiments of love. She was,
is now. What a danger, this looking always
for detail in paths of children, lilac, forsythia,
each field exploding into root and stalk,
tassel and ant, forests yielding trees,
my mother's face shattering into fine lines,
veins on the backs of her hands, her wrist
ticking, ticking. Take one step closer to light
and you yourself become the stranger.

Lecture to the Bioscience Class: Pine and Lightning, Cataclysm and Stone

Life's dirt-cheap: at least 10 trillion ants
in the world, a thousand living creatures
in every human abode, not counting the thousand mites.
Yet the only life we're given we must bear
all our days like a candle through a drafty mansion,
one tear-shaped drop of salty blood in the sea,
a single scent to track through forests
rioting with pollen, blood-spore, paths
of carnivore and prey, carrion and compost,
leaf-mold, mushroom, wildflower, pine.
Bristlecone pines are with us 5000 years.
Some coal seams, touched off by lightning,
have been smoldering 2000 years. Likewise
some passions, our priceless inheritance, urge
to fly, to war, heartfelt aching just to love,
to dream our age away. Lightning can attain
30,000°, earth's core still molten, glowing hot
as Sol. While we come in time to know such heat,
we're made to cool and cool since fragile hearts and lungs
can't withstand, for all our steaming dreams,
such light. The seas float on rock that floats
on seas of molten fire. Continents adrift, we come
together with a force so great we raise
the thunder, a range of jagged mountains
great as myth. 60,000 years it rained to fill
the seas. 950 years were given to Noah. A cup
of tears, just enough to grow a fist of thorns,
a plot of dandelion and crabgrass the best we can
hope for in our brief time. Still we thirst.
Every month the Sahara marches one-half mile south,
and the magic fountain that spouts inside us loses
an inch of its force, as we move a shade closer
to shadow, each bone growing cold.

The Sea of Kansas, Ohio Tundra, Time
Still Running Out

Kansas one million centuries ago, a tropical sea
steaming buoyantly enough to float the ichthyosaur
while mammoths hunting stunted shrubs thunder over
Ohio's rutted tundra, their breath eternal winter.
We're born to new topography, but still this earth
spins us between trajectories of ice and burning,
apogee and perigee of the perilous trek. On Venus
there's heat enough to melt lead, cook the heart.
On Mars, blood would shatter into crimson snow.
There's no place else we can be, in truth, creatures
lusting for moderation, drifting above
the temperate wrack and barm of uterine seas, struggling
up generation's beach to reach solid ground, each fist
an eon of weather, each corpse a tangle of roots.
Passing those who couldn't catch their breath, faces
blue as mountain sky, we know we're not home free.
Burning our histories by barrel and ton, exhaling
our every greed, we've filled the air with CO_2, 23% more
than our parents' parents knew. The very rain corrodes.
How much longer can the children hold their breath?
Plants have saved us so far, green Christs to eat
our sin. Miracles of transubstantiation.
All up and down the street oak and elm, elder and ash
rise to full height, breathing, breathing, nettle and shrub,
redbud and shagbark, weed-blades thrusting up
to shatter concrete, each leap from root to seed
to bloom to fruit our diastole, systole,
each green plot our Eden, time still running out.

The History of Wood

> *It is possible that we appreciate the shapes of trees because of a memory rooted in our most primitive past.*—Science Digest

To begin, we're planed from the grain
of the marriage bed's headboard, lathed
from one of its four posts, and dropped
into cradle or crib, maple bars
between us and earth's abrupt hurt,

to teach us dark from light. Then
we ride with Mother in the rocking chair
or alone on hobbyhorse or swing, curve
of breast and runner, creaking tautness
of chain ensuring a back to every forth.

Later we fall in pairs into the shadow
of some monolithic elm or bedroom wall,
our names a growl and moan, the timbre
of two voices echoing from us in circles,
each year together a work of art,

love's burning bush that can't be consumed.

On the Nature of the Beast

Countless are the patronymics of the countless tribes.
God made Adam different enough to want names named:
Noah's twos, Pharoah's toads and flies, lambs enough
to keep hating angels from lintels of the chosen.
Peter's crowing cock. To Hindus cows are holy hunger,
and Jains sweep roads before them as they go, so not
to harm ant or worm. Parsees summon vultures to undress
their dead. To ancient Greeks, lightning made the bull
and bulls were made to love. For early Christians,
God was finned, gilled, the pelican who bleeds to feed
its young. Francis called his body Brother Ass.
Joseph of Cupertino flapped scrawny arms and soared,
sparrow trilling above the altar fires. Mary discovered
the divinity dwelling in a stable. At revivals
in primeval Kentucky, believers fell to all fours,
lifted hind legs, sniffed and scratched as they gathered
at the foot of the oldest oak to tree the demon.
Shakers danced in roiling files, sexes apart, the thunder
in the upper room, chanting *Hiss, hiss, hiss, chain
the Devil*. At the Full Gospel Jesus Church
in Logan, West Virginia, worshippers try in the tangle
of gleaming diamondback and copperhead to untie knots
that bind them to their humanity, weight and ache
of memory. Such heart-work brews from blood and sweat
the wine of believing, erects chapels of bone modeled
on the master template, skin hairy and weathered,
stretched taut enough to drum out every heart's report,
chirp and bray, shriek and baa, baa, beetle-click,
neigh and hoot of whale, monkey-rraup, each thought
drowned in roaring, *Homo sapiens* seeking wonders
of invisible worlds, souls pent in bone cages,
to reveal what perfect animals we are.

Einstein, Placenta, the Caves of Lascaux

The natural universe moves to precise rhythms:
Einstein died at 1:15 a.m. E.S.T. on April 18, 1955,
while speaking frantic German to a New Jersey nurse
who, though she knew only English, still comprehended
two hands seizing the sheets, the jaw stricken slack,
eyes turning up zeros. Each percentage point rise
in the annual national unemployment rate produces
an additional 320 suicides. Nature works in five ways:
gravity (through the agency of the as-yet-undiscovered,
the graviton), electromagnetism (which can be explained
only by assuming that the energy of each photon
equals the frequency of the light multiplied
by Planck's constant h), the strong force (gluons),
the weak force (the Z and W particles we've only just found),
and the human force (or belief), so powerful after all
that it can for example propel women and men
through the exact replica of the caves of Lascaux
of the Aurignacio-Perigordian period (c.14,000–c.13,500 B.C.)
located a stone's throw from the real Paleolithic thing
already damaged irreparably by the same force.
All such movements of matter into energy, energy to matter
are of course influenced by what we know of love and fear,
as when, for example, in my twelfth grade biology class
in Cleveland at St. Ignatius High School
when the Jesuit instructor tossed onto the lab table
the still warm placenta bloody as sunrise
in its clear plastic bag, eight youngsters, 1/3 of the class,
left the lab and ran directly to the room marked *Men*.

The Bird Graveyard

In Germany, the legend goes, there's a bird
that sings so true a monk once stood listening
beneath a linden tree for forty years
and thought it was but an hour. Birds were made
because the silence, which already was,
would in time have made the Maker mad. Sit watching,
thinking before any window. Can there be
a better idea than the song sparrow flitting
from twig to twig? Dawn's a raven dying,
night a flock of starlings wheeling to cover
the sun. No creatures are more innocent.
Singing they must always say their names,
a perfect witnessing, nothing but the truth.
But who has seen their corpses in numbers
approaching what must be, given
the countless melodies, the voices of one spring?
I dream of a secret place the birds seek out
when they sense they're failing, growing
mute in time, hearts slowing to cadences
more suited to humans. In this burial ground
no woman or man must ever see
are mountains and valleys filled with trees,
lakes that mirror each cloud scudding past.
And though the sun climbs high each day to roost
in pine and ash, weeping willow and elder,
there's little color. Only tiny bones
in numberless piles beneath each tree
and silence.